God Is

OTHER BOOKS

Dragon Riders of Osnen

Trial by Sorcery
A Bond of Flame
The Warrior's Call
The Coin of Souls
Wing of Terror
Eyes of Stone
Tooth and Claw
The Servant of Souls
Smoke and Shadow
The Dark Rider

Marked by the Dragon

Scale of the Dragon
Egg of the Dragon
Call of the Dragon
Wrath of the Dragon

The Fallen King Chronicles

Dragonsphere
The Fallen King
The Valiant King
The Restored King

Dragons of Isentol

Throne of Deceit
Rune Marked
Empire of Serpents

God Is

RICHARD FIERCE

God Is

Copyright © 2013 by Richard Fierce

Scripture quotations taken from The Holy Bible, New International Version® NIV®

Copyright 1973 1978 1984 2011 by Biblica, Inc. TM

Used by permission. All rights reserved worldwide.

Cover design by germancreative

Dragonfire Press

e-Book ISBN: 978-1-947329-03-4

Print ISBN: 978-1-958354-02-5

Second Edition: 2022

To God

Without Him, this would never have been written.

AWESOME

Despite our best efforts and our most eloquent words, we are woefully inadequate when we attempt to describe God. And it's simply because He is *so* awesome.

Psalm 33:6-9 says, "By the word of the Lord the heavens were made, their starry host by the breath of his mouth. He gathers the waters of the sea into jars; he puts the deep into storehouses. Let all the earth fear the Lord; let all the people of the world revere him. For he spoke, and it came to be; he commanded, and it stood firm."

By His word alone, without lifting a finger, God created the heavens and breathed the stars into existence. Do you know how big a star is? Our sun is a star and scientists have said it is 875,000 miles across. Its radius is 435,000 miles. In comparison, the circumference of the Earth is only 40,000 miles which makes our planet roughly 100 times smaller than the sun.

As if that wasn't hard enough to wrap your mind around, consider the fact that our sun isn't even the largest star in space. There is one star called Canis Majoris and it is so enormous, you could fit between 5.8 to 9.2 *billion* of our suns inside of it. And God breathed the stars into existence. I think this not only demonstrates the awesomeness of God, but also shows us that we don't accurately view God. He is so much bigger than we can fathom.

Isaiah 40:12 says, "Who has measured the waters in the hollow of His hand, and marked off the heavens by the span, and calculated the dust of the earth by the measure, and weighed the mountains in a balance, and the hills in a pair of scales?"

A span is the distance measured by a human hand, from the tip of the thumb to the tip of the little finger. In ancient times, a span was considered to be half a cubit. If scientists don't even know how big the universe is, and God measured it with the span of His hand, how big do you think God is?

God didn't just create everything, He also sustains it. We wouldn't have air to breathe, gravity to hold us to the world, or the ability to think without the awesome power of God. Let that sink in for a moment.

Now think about how you use the word awesome. I'm sure we all abuse that word. I know I'm guilty of it. We use it to describe movies, songs, and even speakers. Words are powerful, and more often than not we take them for granted. We use words that don't match what we are describing.

The dictionary defines awesome as: *awe inspiring, showing or characterized by awe*. I highly doubt the things we attribute as being awesome really instill awe in us. We have taken a word meant for something special and made it common place. Just as many of us have made God something common place in our lives—instead of the essential, driving purpose of our lives. When you think about God, awesome should be one of the first words that come to mind.

God is awesome.

That sounds cliché, like something you would see

on a T-shirt or a bumper sticker. But the truth of that statement is an amazing revelation. God is the creator and sustainer of everything. God is omnipresent, meaning He is in all places at all times. He is omnipotent, unlimited and all powerful. The word *is* doesn't seem like much, just two small letters put together. But it is present tense. It doesn't mean was, or will be. It means is. Is is is. God *is* awesome. Constant, present, unchanging.

If a simple movie instills awe in you, you need to raise your expectations. Massively. God is the only one who deserves to have awesome attributed to Him. Exodus 15:11 says:

"Who among the gods

is like you Lord?

who is like you—

majestic in holiness,

awesome in glory,

working wonders?"

The fact that God brought everything we see into existence by simply breathing it should instill in us a deep feeling of awe. Yet sometimes our minds don't quite grasp the amazing revelation of that fact.

So I have a few things I'd like to show you from both the Bible and science that testify to how awesome our God is.

Time

God is not bound by the laws of time and space as we comprehend them. He existed outside of these laws before he created them, after all. And to show that he is not bound by time and space, I am going to show you something amazing from the book of Exodus. Chapter 33:17-23 is a well-known part of the Bible. It says:

"And the Lord said to Moses, "I will do the very thing you have asked, because I am pleased with you and I know you by name." Then Moses said, "Now show me your glory."

And the Lord said, "I will cause all my goodness to pass in front of you, and I will proclaim my name, the Lord, in your presence. I will have mercy on whom I will have mercy, and I will have compassion on whom I will have compassion. But," he said, "you cannot see my face, for no one may see me and live."

Then the Lord said, "There is a place near me where you may stand on a rock. When my glory passes by, I will put you in a cleft in the rock and cover you with my hand until I have passed by. Then I will remove my hand and you will see my back; but my face must not be seen."

In verse 20, God tells Moses "no one can see me and live." Then, in verse 23, God tells Moses that He will pass by and that Moses would see His back. I wondered about this many times, as it seems like it would be a contradiction. However, when you take the time to study the original Hebrew text, the Scriptures take on a whole new level.

Using Strong's Exhaustive Concordance (which lists every word in the Bible and its meaning in the original language), you can do a word study and learn some amazing things.

In verse 23, the word back in Hebrew is *achar* (pronounced aw-khore'). It is Strong's number 268, which means: afterward, back part hereafter, time to come, without. Before the word back are the words "you will see," which is Strong's number 7200. The Hebrew word is *ra'ah*, or raw-aw, meaning "to see" (literally or figuratively), behold, appear, gaze, look on another, sight of others. So using the Hebrew meanings, the verse reads something like this, "Then I will remove my hand, and you shall see (look on another) my back (hereafter, a time to come)."

Earlier in this chapter, we read that Moses is standing on Mount Sinai. Some theologians state that Mount Sinai is the same mountain Jesus was on when he was transfigured. Since the Bible doesn't specifically state which mountain it was, there's a number of places believed to be location.

Fast forward to the transfiguration of Jesus. Luke 9:28-36 says:

"About eight days after Jesus said this, he took Peter, John and James with him and went up onto a mountain to pray. As he was praying, the appearance of his face changed, and his clothes became as bright as a flash of lightning. Two men, Moses and Elijah, appeared in glorious splendor, talking with Jesus. They spoke about his *departure*, which he was about to bring to fulfillment at Jerusalem. Peter and his companions were very sleepy, but when they became fully awake, they saw his glory and the two men standing with him. As the men were leaving Jesus, Peter said to him, "Master, it is good for us to be here. Let us put up three shelters—one for you, one for Moses and one for Elijah." (He did not know what he was saying.)

While he was speaking, a cloud appeared and

covered them, and they were afraid as they entered the cloud. A voice came from the cloud, saying, "This is my Son, whom I have chosen; listen to him." When the voice had spoken, they found that Jesus was alone. The disciples kept this to themselves and did not tell anyone at that time what they had seen."

The word departure in Greek is exodus, which is from ancient Greek drama for the final scene or departure, especially in tragedy.

I believe God sent Moses forward in time to see Jesus because as Hebrews 1:3 says, "The Son is the radiance of God's glory and the exact representation of his being, sustaining all things by his powerful word. After he had provided purification for sins, he sat down at the right hand of the Majesty in heaven."

I have seen it said by many people that the Bible is merely a story book, or that science is the only "factual" thing you can go on. The unfortunate thing for these people is that they are living in ignorance.

There are many things that scientists have discovered or are still in the process of discovering that have already been plainly stated in Scripture. A few examples are:

During the 20th century, many scientists, including Einstein, thought the universe was static. However, in 1929 astronomer Edwin Hubble showed that distant galaxies were receding from the earth, and the further away they were, the faster they were moving. Einstein admitted his mistake, and today most astronomers agree that space is expanding. The amazing thing is that repeatedly God stated that he stretches out the heavens. (Job 9:8, Jeremiah 51:15, Zechariah 12:1, Isaiah 42:5)

Sir Isaac Newton studied light and discovered that white light is made up of seven colors and can be "parted" and then recombined. Science confirmed this four centuries ago, God declared this in Job 38:24.

Scripture assumed a revolving spherical earth when Jesus said at his return some would be asleep at night and some would be working at daytime activities. This is a clear indication of a revolving earth, with day and night occurring simultaneously.

Genesis tells us that God created man from the dust of the earth. Scientists have discovered that the human body is comprised of some 28 base and trace elements, all of which are found in the earth.

Leviticus 17:11 tells us that blood is the source of life. Until 120 years ago, sick people were usually "bled" and usually died as a result. Today we know that healthy blood is necessary to bring life-giving nutrients to every cell in the body. God declared life was in the blood long before science ever knew its purpose.

Three thousand years ago the Bible described the "paths of the sea." In the 19th century, after reading Psalm 8, Matthew Maury (the father of oceanography) researched and discovered ocean currents that follow specific paths through the seas. Using Maury's data, marine navigators have since reduced by many days the time required to travel the seas.

Scripture

The Bible was written over a period of 1600 years (1500 BC to 100 AD) by approximately 40 different people. While there are many religious books, the Bible is the only one that claims to be the actual words of God. The Bible is the most accurate book ever written. There are many who claim the Bible contains inaccuracies or errors, yet no one can ever produce said errors.

Many historians recorded the same events in Scripture that back up the historical accuracy of the Bible. Historical discoveries are constantly coming to light that continue to support everything the Bible says.

Only an awesome God could accomplish something like that.

FAITHFUL

The dictionary defines a promise as "a declaration that one will do or refrain from doing something specified." Promises are not meant to be broken. They are meant to be kept and honored. God keeps His and He expects us to keep ours. All too often, our words come easy and are often uttered without any thought or sincerity behind them. In the midst of difficult situations, we cry out to God and say things like "help me and I will do whatever you want," or any variation of that statement. *"Whatever you want?"* Do we really mean those words?

In Jeremiah, we find that after Nebuchadnezzar had taken the children of Israel into captivity, he left a remnant of people in the land and appointed Gedaliah governor over the land. Ishmael, who was of royal blood, was offended at the choice of Gedaliah, who was a noble but not from the house of David. In Jeremiah 41, Ishmael conspires against Gedaliah and kills him, along with the Chaldean soldiers who are assigned to him. The remnant of people become fearful of Babylon's anger and retaliation for Ishmael's treachery.

They set out to flee to Egypt and as they are traveling, they stop and ask advice of the prophet Jeremiah. We read in Jeremiah 42:1-3 "Then all the army officers, including Johanan the son of Kareah and Jezaniah the son of Hoshaiah, and all the people from the least to the greatest approached Jeremiah the prophet and said to him, "Please, hear our petition and pray to the LORD your God for this entire remnant. For as you now see, though we were once many, now only a few are left. Pray that the LORD your God will tell us the where we should go and what we should do."

A promise made

Jeremiah 42:4-6 says, "I have heard you," replied Jeremiah, "May the LORD be a true and faithful witness against us if we do not act in accordance with everything the LORD your God sends you to tell us. Whether it is favorable or unfavorable, we will obey the LORD our God, to whom we are sending you, so that it will go well with us, for we will obey the LORD our God."

They came to Jeremiah asking for counsel when they had already decided to flee to Egypt. A person asking for advice should always be honest and not have a predetermined course of action or agenda.

"Whether favorable or unfavorable, we will obey the LORD our God." As believers, we should embody that statement. Even though it may be contrary to our feelings or desires, we should always embrace what God requires and commands. Far too many serve God out of convenience as long as what God wants is what they want. We need to be willing to obey His voice no matter what.

Joshua 24:24 says "And the people said to Joshua, "We will serve the LORD our God and obey him." Deuteronomy 27:10 says, "Obey the LORD your

God and follow his commands and decrees that I give you today."

Sometimes it isn't easy to smile, be polite, put others first, or do the Father's will, especially when we are tired, feeling our worst, or even in an uncaring mood. But it wasn't easy for Jesus to climb Calvary's hill, either.

God will hold us accountable for our words, so remember that before you speak. Ecclesiastes 5:1-7 says, "Guard your steps when you go to the house of God. Go near to listen rather than to offer the sacrifice of fools, who do not know that they do wrong. Do not be quick with your mouth, do not be hasty in your heart to utter *anything* before God. God is in heaven and you are on earth, so let your words be few. A dream comes when there are many cares, and many words mark the speech of a fool. When you make a vow to God, do not delay to fulfill it. He has no pleasure in fools; fulfill your vow. It is better not to make a vow than to make one and not fulfill it. Do not let your mouth lead you into sin. And do not protest to the temple messenger, "My vow was a mistake." Why should God be angry at what you say and destroy the work of your hands? Much dreaming and many words are meaningless. Therefore fear God."

I have heard a lot of people tell others to just speak to God and say whatever comes to mind. But Scripture tells us otherwise.

A promise broken

When Jeremiah returns with God's answer, he gives them two options. Chapter 42 verses nine through twelve say:

42:9-12: "He said to them, "This is what the Lord, the God of Israel, to whom you sent me to present your petition, says: 'If you stay in this land, I will build you up and not tear you down; I will plant you and not uproot you, for I have relented concerning the disaster I have inflicted on you. Do not be afraid of the king of Babylon, whom you now fear. Do not be afraid of him, declares the Lord, for I am with you and will save you and deliver you from his hands. I will show you compassion so that he will have compassion on you and restore you to your land.'

42:13-17: "However, if you say, 'We will not stay in this land,' and so disobey the Lord your God, and if you say, 'No, we will go and live in Egypt, where we will not see war or hear the trumpet or be hungry for bread,' then hear the word of the Lord, you remnant of Judah. This is what the Lord Almighty, the God of Israel, says: 'If you are determined to go to Egypt and you do go to settle there, then the sword you fear will overtake you there, and the famine you dread will follow you into Egypt, and there you will die. Indeed, all who are determined to go to Egypt to settle there will die by the sword, famine and plague; not one of them will survive or escape the disaster I will bring on them.'"

God says if they stay, the Babylonians will have mercy on them. And if they leave, the sword, famine, and pestilence will pursue them. Obey God and be blessed or disobey and deal with God's anger.

People's reactions never cease to amaze me when

the answers they seek don't come back the way they expect. Despite their promise to obey God, Jeremiah 43:7 tells us, "So they entered Egypt in disobedience to the Lord and went as far as Tahpanhes."

They blatantly rejected their promise and chose their own way. The remnant of people conducted themselves as most of us do today. We will serve God so long as everything goes our way. We should always persist and keep God's commands whether it is convenient or not and whether He blesses us or not. Job summed it up perfectly in Job 13:15 when he said, "Though He slay me, yet will I trust in Him."

The remnant said whether good or bad they would obey God's voice, yet they blasphemed God and took His name in vain by breaking their promise. When we say we will do something and then fail to do it, we dishonor God's name. Promise keeping honors Him. Not keeping our word takes God's name in vain.

Unfortunately, many people make promises to God with no intention of keeping them unless it benefits them. We live in an era of unkept promises. Nations sign treaties and then break them at will. Couples show little regard for their wedding vows.

The brilliant Christian scholar and writer C. S. Lewis took that truth seriously. He was determined to pay what he had vowed. His biography tells of the suffering he endured because he kept a promise he had made to a friend during World War I. This friend was worried about the care of his wife and small daughter if he should be killed in battle, so Lewis assured him that if that were to happen he would look after them. As the war dragged on, the man was killed. True to his word, Lewis took care of his friend's family. Yet no matter how helpful he tried to be, the woman was ungrateful, rude, arrogant, and domineering. Through it all, Lewis kept forgiving her. He refused to let her actions become an excuse to renege on his promise.

Here's an interesting story for you: A man named Russell Edward Herman left trillions of dollars to thousands of people he'd never met. What was the catch? Russell Edward Herman didn't have trillions of dollars. He was just a simple, poor carpenter. While the wild, wild will of the late Russell Herman never paid off for his "beneficiaries," it certainly enlivened conversations. Take the tiny Ohio River town of Cave-In-Rock, for example. Herman bequeathed $2.41 billion to them. Cave-In-Rock's mayor, Albert Kaegi had this to say, "It's an odd thing to happen, isn't it?" While the will would never pay off, the mayor had no trouble imagining uses for the willed imaginary monies. Russell Edward Herman had great intentions, but he lacked the resources needed to make them a reality.

The greatness of God, however, stands in sharp contrast. God not only has made great and precious promises, He has the ability and power to follow through on every single one of them.

Result of a broken promise

Unfortunately for the remnant, the Egyptian gods would provide no refuge.

Jeremiah 43:9-12 says, "While the Jews are

watching, take some large stones with you and bury them in clay in the brick pavement at the entrance to Pharaoh's palace in Tahpanhes. Then say to them, 'This is what the Lord Almighty, the God of Israel, says: I will send for my servant Nebuchadnezzar king of Babylon, and I will set his throne over these stones I have buried here; he will spread his royal canopy above them. He will come and attack Egypt, bringing death to those destined for death, captivity to those destined for captivity, and the sword to those destined for the sword. He will set fire to the temples of the gods of Egypt; he will burn their temples and take their gods captive. As a shepherd picks his garment clean of lice, so he will pick Egypt clean and depart.'"

The world cannot offer refuge from the chastising hand of God. Disobedience has a cost, a cost sometimes more drastic than the cost of obedience.

Jeremiah 44:24-28 continues, "Then Jeremiah said to all the people, including the women, "Hear the word of the Lord, all you people of Judah in Egypt. This is what the Lord Almighty, the God of Israel, says: You and your wives have done what you said you would do when you promised, 'We will certainly carry out the vows we made to burn incense and pour out drink offerings to the Queen of Heaven.'

"Go ahead then, do what you promised! Keep your vows! But hear the word of the Lord, all you Jews living in Egypt: 'I swear by my great name,' says the Lord, 'that no one from Judah living anywhere in Egypt will ever again invoke my name or swear, "As surely as the Sovereign Lord lives." For I am watching over them for harm, not for good; the Jews in Egypt will perish by sword and famine until they are all destroyed. Those who escape the sword and return to the land of Judah from Egypt will be very few. Then the whole remnant of Judah who came to live in Egypt will know whose word will stand—mine or theirs.'"

Hebrews 12 gives us great insight into God's chastisement. Verse 6 says, "My son, do not make light of the Lord's discipline, and do not lose heart when he rebukes you, because the Lord disciplines the one he loves, and he chastens everyone he accepts as his son."

Verse 11 also explains, "No discipline seems pleasant at the time, but painful. Later on, however, it produces a harvest of righteousness and peace for those who have been trained by it."

As believers, we need to understand that God both blesses obedience and disciplines disobedience in us as His children.

I share all this to show that man is not faithful. Yet despite our unfaithfulness, God remains faithful to us. How many promises do you think the Bible contains? A hundred? A thousand? According to Dr. Reginald Dunlap, there are approximately thirty thousand. 30,000!

Peter wrote about the promises of God. 2 Peter 1:3-4 says, "His divine power has given us everything we need for a godly life through our knowledge of him who called us by his own glory and goodness. Through these he has given us his very great and precious promises, so that through them you may participate in the divine nature, having escaped the corruption in the world caused by evil desires."

Peter called them *precious* promises. He used it at least 5 times in his two books: precious faith 1

Peter 1:7, 2 Peter 1:1, precious blood 1 Peter 1:19, precious stone 1 Peter 2:4-6, precious Lord 1 Peter 2:7 and precious promises 2 Peter 1:4. What is it that makes them so great and precious? Because they come from a great God who can do the impossible and because they lead to an abundant life.

Below are some verses that declare God's faithfulness.

Numbers 23:19: "God is not a man, that he should lie, nor a son of man, that he should change his mind. Does he speak and then not act? Does he *promise* and not fulfill?"

1 Kings 8:56: "Praise be to the LORD, who has given rest to his people Israel just as he promised. Not one word has failed of all the good *promises* he gave through his servant Moses.

Joshua 21:45: "Not one of all the LORD's good *promises* to the house of Israel failed; every one was fulfilled."

Joshua 23:14: "Now I am about to go the way of all the earth. You know with all your heart and soul that not one of all the good *promises* the LORD your God gave you has failed. Every *promise* has been fulfilled; not one has failed."

2 Peter 3:9: "The Lord is not slow in keeping his

promise, as some understand slowness. He is patient with you, not wanting anyone to perish, but everyone to come to repentance."

Hebrews 10:23: "Let us hold unswervingly to the hope we profess, for he who promised is *faithful*."

Deuteronomy 7:9: "Know therefore that the Lord your God is God; he is the *faithful God*, keeping his covenant of love to a thousand generations of those who love him and keep his commandments."

Deuteronomy 32:4: "He is the Rock, his works are perfect, and all his ways are just.

A *faithful God* who does no wrong, upright and just is he."

Psalm 33:4: "For the word of the Lord is right and true; he is *faithful* in all he does."

Psalm 86:15: "But you, Lord, are a compassionate and gracious God, slow to anger, abounding in love and *faithfulness*."

Psalm 117:2: "For great is his love toward us, and the *faithfulness* of the Lord endures forever."

Psalm 145:13: "Your kingdom is an everlasting kingdom, and your dominion endures through all generations. The Lord is trustworthy in all he *promises* and *faithful* in all he does."

Lamentations 3:23: "Because of the Lord's great love we are not consumed, for his compassions never fail. They are new every morning; great is your *faithfulness*."

1 Corinthians 1:8-9: "He will also keep you firm to the end, so that you will be blameless on the day of our Lord Jesus Christ. *God is faithful*, who has called you into fellowship with his Son, Jesus Christ our Lord."

2 Thessalonians 3:3: "But the *Lord is faithful*, and he will strengthen you and protect you from the evil one."

1 Corinthians 10:13: "No temptation has overtaken you except what is common to mankind. And *God is faithful*; he will not let you be tempted beyond what you can bear. But when you are tempted, he will also provide a way out so that you can endure it."

Here's an amazing revelation: Peter says that claiming these precious promises makes us "participators" with Christ. A participator is defined as someone who takes part in or shares with others. We can claim these promises when we become a follower of Jesus. When we partner with Christ, we become like him. This new nature, however, is not automatic. We must flee or "escape" the corruption of this world. That is why in the following verse Peter describes the great effort we must put forth to add to our faith all kinds of godly characteristics.

God's promises

Considering how many promises are in the Bible, it would take an incredible amount of time to go over each one. I will share a few, however, as I believe these are very important to today.

I will build the church.

Jesus said that he would build his church and the gates of hell would not prevail against it (Matthew 16:18). As believers, we are a part of this church that Jesus built. It has been in existence for over 2000 years and will remain until the end. The church has certainly been attacked from within and without as Satan continues to try to destroy it, but Jesus *promised* the gates would not prevail.

I will be with you.

God has promised to be with his people numerous times throughout history. In Joshua 1:5, he said, "No one will be able to stand against you all the days of your life. As I was with Moses, so I will be with you; I will never leave you nor forsake you."

In the Great Commission, Jesus said, "And surely I will be with you always, to the very end of the age." (Matthew 28:20)

Paul wrote to Timothy, saying, "At my first

defense, no one came to my support, but everyone deserted me. May it not be held against them. But the Lord stood at my side and gave me strength, so that through me the message might be fully proclaimed and all the Gentiles might hear it. And I was delivered from the lion's mouth." (2 Timothy 4:16-17)

God promises his presence. He stays close to us, and even when we are in dark times in life, He is always with us.

I will pour out my Spirit.

God also promised to "pour out His Spirit". That promise was spoken by prophets for centuries and finally came to pass on the day of Pentecost when the church began. He promises the Holy Spirit to those who put their faith in Christ. Ephesians 1:13-14 says, "And you also were included in Christ when you heard the message of truth, the gospel of your salvation. When you believed, you were marked in him with a seal, the promised Holy Spirit, who is a deposit guaranteeing our inheritance until the redemption of those who are God's possession—to the praise of his glory."

How amazing is it that we have God's Spirit dwelling in us to lead us, comfort us, strengthen us, and pray for us? (Romans 8:26)

I will come again.

John 14:1-3 says, "Do not let your hearts be troubled. You believe in God; believe also in me. My Father's house has many rooms; if that were not so, would I have told you that I am going there to prepare a place for you? And if I go and prepare a place for you, I will come back and take you to be with me that you also may be where I am."

These few are not the only *precious* promises, no doubt I could list hundreds more. But my hope is that these few would ignite an excitement in us and cause us to appreciate God and His ability and power to keep His word.

Receiving God's promises

In order to claim the promises God has given us, we must first know what they are. Prayerful study of the Scripture will reveal a treasure of wisdom, but also reveal His promises to us as his children.

There's a story of a little girl who pointed to a Bible laying on a bookshelf and asks whose it is. The mother answers, "That's God's book." The little girl thinks a moment, then says: "Shouldn't we give it back to him? No one ever reads it."

Sadly, this is the truth in many households of believers. We have the Bible, God's revelation of himself to mankind, and yet we don't read it, seeing it as more of a duty to study it than a privilege. How can we know what God says if we don't read his Word?

I strongly believe that is why so many Christians fall away from the faith. They believe what other people wrongly teach about God and his church. Prosperity preaching, false doctrines, the list goes on and on. In 2 Corinthians 1:20, Paul says: "For no matter how many promises God has made, they are "Yes" in Christ. And so through him the "Amen" is spoken by us to the glory of God."

Patience.

It is our nature to want things quickly and on our timelines. But there are countless times when God made a promise and it did not come to pass for many years. Take Abraham for example. God promised Abraham a son from his own loins even though he was old and his wife Sarah was barren. Abraham was 75 years old when God told him he would be the father of many nations.

He was 100 when his son Isaac was born. Abraham waited *25 years* for God's promise to be fulfilled.

David is another example of being patient for God's promises. He was anointed as the next king of Israel when he was a young shepherd (1 Samuel 16:11-13). He was between the ages of 12 and 15. 2 Samuel 5:4 tells us that David was crowned king at the age of 30. David waited at least fifteen years for God's promise. God promised the Messiah to Adam and Eve in the book of Genesis, yet it was centuries later before it happened. God works in his own time. Waiting is not easy, but we must learn to be patient or we will miss God's promises. Do not mistake His delay for denial. And changing a promise is not breaking a promise. God can change a temporal promise into a spiritual promise.

Obedience.

An important aspect of receiving God's promises is being obedient to His will. Hebrews 10:36 tells us, "You need to persevere so that when you have done the will of God, you will receive what he has promised." Some promises are also conditional. We must fulfill our responsibilities before we get the rewards of His promises. The greatest promise is salvation and eternal life. We don't get this automatically, but through accepting that Jesus is Lord and repenting.

Faith.

This is the big one. Faith is what drives it all. Hebrews 11:1 says, "Faith is confidence in what we hope for and assurance about what we do not see." Also consider Hebrews 11:6: "And without *faith* it is impossible to please God, because anyone who comes to him must *believe* that he exists and that he *rewards* those who earnestly seek him."

Paul explained it simply in 2 Corinthians 5:7. "For we live by faith, not by sight." By faith, as difficult as it seems sometimes, we trust in an invisible God and stand on His promises. Being a person of faith doesn't mean we don't doubt, it means that we believe more than we doubt.

PROVIDER

God understands our needs

When we are in need or when we lack something that we consider to be essential to our well-being, our first temptation is to think that God has forgotten us; that He is unaware or unconcerned about our welfare. This is especially true if the need is longstanding.

So when, and if, we pray, our prayers take on a petulant, complaining tone. Instead of asking God to meet the need, we demand to know why He isn't meeting our need. We may pray repeatedly, not necessarily because we don't have the faith, but perhaps for other reasons. Impatience, or perhaps a fear that He isn't listening to us. And so we nag Him. If you have children, you know what I mean.

"Can I have some candy? When can I have it? I want it now, I don't want to wait." Sometimes husbands and wives do this as well. Why? They're just not sure that they're getting through or that they're being heard. She's not convinced that her husband really comprehends how essential it is that he fix the toilet. And the noncommittal grunts that she receives when she brings it up are not reassuring.

Matthew 15:32-38 says:

"Jesus called his disciples to him and said, "I have compassion for these people; they have already been with me three days and have nothing to eat. I do not want to send them away hungry, or they may collapse on the way." His disciples answered, "Where could we get enough bread in this remote place to feed such a crowd?" "How many loaves do you have?" Jesus asked. "Seven," they replied, "and a few small fish." He told the crowd to sit down on the ground. Then he took the seven loaves and the fish, and when he had given thanks, he broke them and gave them to the disciples, and they in turn to the people. They all ate and were satisfied. Afterward the disciples picked up seven basketfuls of broken pieces that were left over. The number of those who ate was four thousand, besides women and children.

Verse 32 tells us that when God doesn't provide what we feel we need, it isn't due to a lack of caring or a lack of knowing. It may be because our understanding of our needs is inadequate. Perhaps He has something better in store for us. It may be because the timing isn't right. It may be because God wants to develop patience or faith. It may be for reasons we can't understand. But we don't need to nag or badger Him to get His attention. Not only does He know, He cares.

Earlier in the book of Matthew, Jesus is teaching the disciples to pray. He said, "And when you pray, do not keep on babbling like pagans, for they think they will be heard because of their many words. Do not be like them, for your Father knows what you need before you ask him." (Matthew 6:7-8)

God meets our needs

God does not just know what we need, He provides it as well. Do you trust Him to provide what you need? Who are you depending on to meet your needs? When you think about how the bills are going to get paid, how the refrigerator is going to be filled, how the children are going to be clothed, what does your mind rest upon as the source for meeting those needs. Look at the disciples' reaction in verse 33 and 34:

"His disciples answered, "Where could we get enough bread in this remote place to feed such a crowd?" "How many loaves do you have?" Jesus asked. "Seven," they replied, "and a few small fish."

The possibility that Jesus could meet the need seems to never have entered their minds. The need is so great, and their understanding of Jesus' power so small, that they do not look to Him. Instead, they look to themselves: "Where could *we* get enough bread?" Isn't it the same with us? When you are faced with an unexpected need, how do you respond? Do you immediately pray, "Lord, how are you going to meet this need?" Or do you respond like the disciples: "How will I do this?"

What was the result of looking to themselves? Most likely discouragement. They considered all the factors; the remoteness of the location, the size of the crowd, the lack of their resources—and they concluded they could not meet the need.

What happens to us when we react like the disciples? You may get discouraged, panicked even. On the other hand, you may not, at least in the short run. If you are very competent and resourceful, you may do fine for a long while. When needs arise, you manage to find a way to meet them. You take pride in the fact that you are on top of every situation, prepared for every eventuality. Somehow, you always manage to find a way through any difficulty. You are convinced that you have no need of God or anyone else. But in reality, you are desperately poor in the one thing that matters most—fellowship with Christ.

Eventually, you will face death, and none of your resources will be able to help you. There are many possible sources we can rely on to meet our needs—ourselves, the government, an employer, a husband or wife, family or friends; your intelligence, your degree, your skills, your reputation, your money—and that's somewhat acceptable as long as we realize that those things are not really the source, but only a conduit of God's provision. They're just intermediaries. Our ultimate trust and reliance must be in God Himself. Anyone or anything else will ultimately fail.

God meets our needs through others

Jesus could have met this need in any number of ways. He could have simply caused their hunger to abate. He could have caused bread and fish to appear in each person's lap. He could have turned stones into bread. He could have caused bread to drop out of the sky. He could have produced bread and fish himself.

Instead, Jesus chose to use what was offered by the disciples and make it adequate to meet the need.

In the same way, God generally meets our needs through one another.

"Share with God's people who are in need." (Romans 12:13)

"At the present time your plenty will supply what they need, so that in turn their plenty will supply what you need." (2 Corinthians 8:14)

"You will be enriched in every way so that you can be generous on every occasion, and through us your generosity will result in thanksgiving to God." (2 Corinthians 9:11)

These verses clearly teach that God gives us wealth and possessions, not merely to bless us, but also to enable us to meet the needs of others. We are trustees of God's gifts, not owners, and God intends that we should seek out opportunities to share those gifts with others.

This requires both generosity and humility. Those who have the resources must be willing to give, and those who lack must be willing to receive (and make their needs known). How do we do this? Be sensitive to those who may be in need of financial help; assist them personally or make their needs known to the pastors. Seek out opportunities to meet needs through the gift of other resources—time, abilities, encouragement, use of assets (car, snow blower). Give generously and without complaint, knowing that everything you have comes from God.

God meets our needs to reveal the gospel

Jesus answered, "I tell you the truth, you are looking for me, not because you saw miraculous signs but because you ate the loaves and had your fill. Do not work for food that spoils, but for food that endures to eternal life, which the Son of Man will give you. On him God the Father has placed his seal of approval." ... Then Jesus declared, "I am the bread of life. He who comes to me will never go hungry, and he who believes in me will never be thirsty." (John 6:26-27, 35)

The intent of the feeding miracles was to illustrate the source of life, just as bread is the source of physical life. Christ cares for our temporary physical needs—our earthly bodily life—in order to show that He has the power to care for our souls and to give us eternal life.

Are you trusting in Him to give you that life?

HEALER

Jehovah Rapha.

The Lord that heals. This name is first revealed shortly after the Israelites were released from their bondage in Egypt. They passed through the Red Sea and made it to the other side. The people were so excited to finally be free that they immediately started praising God. Exodus 15 verses 1-3 records the song:

"I will sing to the LORD, for he is highly exalted. The horse and its rider he has hurled into the sea. The LORD is my strength and my song; he has become my salvation. He is my God, and I will praise him, my father's God, and I will exalt him. The LORD is a warrior; the LORD is his name." God is referred to by two of his names in these verses: Elohim and Yahweh.

Their praising quickly turns into a time of complaining. In verse 22, we read that Moses led the Israelites into the Desert of Shur. Shur means wall. And I'm sure that they felt as though they had run into a wall of despair instead of a window of blessing. Some of us have felt like that at times. After wandering in the wilderness for three days with no water, the people turn on Moses at a place called Marah, which means bitterness. This is the same name Naomi chose for herself in Ruth 1:20 after experiencing incredible pain and disappointment.

They finally found water, but much to their disappointment it had a very bitter taste. In verse 24, they put Moses on the spot and ask, "What are we to drink?" The Israelites were angry with God but took it out on a person. I'm sure we have all done that at some point. I know I have. We tend to take things out on others when we don't get what we want when we want it.

When we get excited everything seems great but then there is the inevitable let-down. The Israelites saw God get them through the Red Sea, but now they are thirsty and have a bitter taste in their mouth. You may feel that way right now as you read this book (hopefully not from the book). You've had high expectations and gone to great disappointment and heavy discouragement.

It is interesting how gratitude turns into whining when the memory of God's faithfulness gets somehow forgotten in the things of life. Only three days had passed and they went from singing God's praises to being in a ditch of despair. Bitterness can blind us to the promises of God. They had forgotten that life in Egypt was terrible even though they ate bitter herbs as part of the Passover to remember the bitterness of slavery (Exodus 12:8). Freedom from Egypt had also left them feeling bitter because their expectations were shattered.

And so Moses did what we should all do; he cried out to God. Instead of protesting, he prays. That's what difficulty can do for us. It can cause us to realize we can't do everything in our own power.

God answers Moses by showing him a simple piece of wood. Moses takes the wood and whips it into the water which causes the water to becomes sweet. God then initiates a test and tells them in verse 26: "If you listen carefully to the voice of the LORD your God and do what is right in his eyes, if you pay attention to his commands and keep all his decrees, I will not bring on you any of the diseases I brought on the Egyptians, for I am the LORD, who heals you." God is linking their holiness with their health as He declares one more name for Himself: Jehovah Rapha. In the midst of their bitterness and hurt, God reveals Himself as their healer.

The word Rapha is used over sixty times in the Old Testament and means, "to restore, to heal, or to cure" physically, emotionally, and spiritually. In 1 Kings 18:30, we get a picture of what Rapha means when we read that Elijah "repaired" (Rapha) the altar of Jehovah. In 2 Kings 2:21, God "heals" (Rapha) the water when Elisha throws salt in the spring. The word has the idea of restoring something to its original state. Sometimes we need healing in all three areas like David did in Psalm 6:2-3:

Have mercy on me, Lord, for I am faint;
heal me, Lord, for my bones are in agony.
My soul is in deep anguish.
How long, Lord, how long?

Emotional—have mercy on me, Lord, for I am faint.

Physical—heal me, Lord, for my bones are in agony.

Spiritual—my soul is in deep anguish.

Sometimes one of these areas is in greater need than the others. God reveals himself as Jehovah Rapha when we are in need.

Emotional Healing

God heals emotional hurts and broken hearts. Psalm 147:3 says: "He heals the brokenhearted and binds up their wounds." The word broken means "to burst, to break into pieces, to crush and to smash." You may feel that way right now. Your emotional pain is overwhelming. Whatever pain you're carrying around, hand it to the Healer today.

You may have unbelievably intense hurt that no one can begin to relate to. Maybe it's something that happened when you were younger. Or perhaps it just happened yesterday. In the midst of your tears, cry out to Jehovah Rapha and ask Him to put you back together again. Related to this, relational ruptures can cause emotional pain. If you're struggling with a broken relationship, I encourage you to do what you can to make peace as Romans 12:18 says, "If it is possible, as far as it depends on you, live at peace with everyone."

A few years ago, my wife and I found out she was pregnant. We were ecstatic. When she was about seven weeks, she started to have pain in her side. She is one tough woman and has a high tolerance for pain. This pain, however, had her crawling on her hands and knees. I told her if the pain was still there in the morning, I was taking her to the doctor. When she woke up from what little sleep she got, she was still hurting.

I drove her to the local urgent care and they ran some tests. The doctor wasn't sure, but he thought she was having a miscarriage. He referred us to a hospital in a nearby city and we drove there. After we were taken into the ultrasound room, the nurse showed us the baby on the screen and we even heard the heartbeat. It was truly an amazing moment and one I will never forget.

The nurse left and came back a short while later. She said the doctor established that the baby was ectopic. In other words, once the egg had been fertilized, it had not rolled down the fallopian tube into the womb. The baby had begun growing in the tube. The reason she was in pain was due to the fact that as the baby was growing, it was causing her to bleed internally. The nurse then informed us that my wife could not leave the hospital because it was deemed a threat to the mother's life.

In one quick moment, our celebrating turned into despair. The urgent care doctor called and told the hospital to release us to see another doctor locally. And so we headed off to see this new doctor who was about to close his office, but said he would see what was going on with my wife.

As we were riding in the car, I was praying that God would miraculously move the baby into the womb. I really believed He would. When we reached the doctor's office, after another ultrasound, he confirmed that the baby was in fact ectopic. He said that she was bleeding internally and her life was at stake. He said the tube, along with the baby, needed to be removed. He quickly transported my wife to surgery and I met them at the hospital across the street.

Everything happened so fast that it wasn't until I was sitting alone in the waiting room that the weight of it all hit me. It was between six and seven in the evening, and with the exception of myself, there wasn't a single person in that room. I felt so helpless and so alone. And then I cried. I cried for my wife, for my unborn baby that I would never get to meet, and I cried for myself.

I prayed the hardest thing I have ever prayed in that moment. I said, "God, whatever happens from all this, I pray that you get glory through it all. You give and you take away, blessed be your name." After surgery, the doctor met me in a side room and said that when he went in to operate, he found that her tubes were scarred and stuck to her ovaries, likely from an infection. He said that it was almost impossible she would ever get pregnant again, and if she did, it would be the same scenario. I felt like someone had just shot me in the heart.

This happened on a Wednesday. My boss gave me the rest of the week off to take care of my wife and it was the most heartbreaking and painful time of our lives. When Sunday came and we went to church, one of the young ladies sang a very powerful song. It's called Healer by Kari Jobe. I can't explain what happened, and neither can my wife, but through our worship that day God healed us emotionally in a way I never imagined possible.

And despite what the doctor said, we are believing God for the impossible.

Physical healing

God heals physical pains and broken bones as well. Maybe you are experiencing a tough time right now because you are in pain, or maybe you've been devastated by the news you've received about a family member or a close friend. At times like this, we need to call out to God to do His healing work in our lives. Scripture is filled with examples of God's healing. In 2 Kings 20:5-6, we read about how Hezekiah became very ill and was about to die.

As a result of intense prayer, he was healed and his life was extended. This is only one example of God's amazing power. In the gospel accounts we see that Jesus spent a lot of time healing people.

I have seen God heal in a powerful way. In 2009, my wife's grandmother on her mother's side was diagnosed with cancer. She went through surgery and chemo sessions in order to get rid of it. After a few weeks of this, she came to church with the family. There happened to be a guest speaker who had a testimony of healing. After the service, her grandmother asked to be prayed over. The pastor anointed her with oil and the entire family, as well as the pastor and the guest speaker, laid hands on her.

The power of the Holy Spirit was so strong that I knew without any doubt she was healed. The pastor told her to share the details of her next doctor's visit with him. On her next visit, the doctor confirmed that all of the cancer cells were gone. It was an amazing display of God's power and grace.

A few weeks later, however, she started feeling sick. She went back to the doctor and he said that she had cancer again, this time in her brain. Sometimes when we defeat Goliath, we have to deal with his brother also. She ended up giving up hope and passed away from the cancer. Yet God did heal her. I believe He could have again if she had asked.

Spiritual healing

This is perhaps the most important aspect of God's healing power. We are spiritually sick and God provides the healing and wholeness we need through the blood of Jesus.

Jeremiah 17:9 says, "The heart is deceitful above all things and beyond cure. Who can understand it?"

We are sinners, inflicted from birth with the disease of death and destruction and in desperate need of healing. Early in his ministry, Jesus went into the synagogue in his hometown of Nazareth and quoted from the Book of Isaiah.

"The Spirit of the Lord is on me, because he has anointed me to proclaim good news to the poor. He has sent me to *proclaim freedom* for the prisoners and recovery of sight for the blind, to set the *oppressed free*, to proclaim the year of the Lord's favor." (Luke 4:18-19)

Once we are set free spiritually, Jesus can break every other bondage we are under, especially addictions and deep sin issues. While it is true Jesus healed a lot of people physically, he was always more concerned about curing the sin problem. Do you remember when John the Baptist sent his disciples to ask Jesus if he was really the Messiah? Do you remember what Jesus said?

"The blind receive sight, the lame walk, those who have leprosy are cured, the deaf hear, the dead are raised, and the *good news is preached* to the poor." (Matthew 11:5)

Evangelism, not just physical healing, is the driving force behind the miracles and should be the main point of our ministries. The pervasiveness of sin in our souls is pictured very vividly in Isaiah 1:5-6: "Why do you persist in rebellion? Your whole head is injured, your whole heart afflicted. From the sole of your foot to the top of your head there is no soundness—only wounds and welts and open sores, not cleansed or bandaged or soothed with oil."

Our depravity is total, affecting every part of our lives. Looking down to verse 18, we see the good news is revealed as the cleansing power of forgiveness: "Though your sins are like scarlet, they shall be as white as snow; though they are red as crimson, they shall be like wool."

Nine Principals

When the Israelites were faced with three days of no water, Numbers 15:25 says that God tested them. Likewise, when we go through tough times emotionally, physically or spiritually, sometimes we are really entering a testing time. There are at least nine principles to keep in mind that will help us pass the test and better understand the healing power of Jehovah Rapha.

1 – Trials and troubles can get us back on track. That's exactly what the psalmist said in Psalm 119:67, 71: "Before I was afflicted I went astray, but now I obey your word … It was good for me to be afflicted so that I might learn your decrees." We all have empty places in our lives as a result of brokenness and dissatisfaction. When we're hurting, we must run to Jehovah Rapha and resist the urge to fill our emptiness with things that will not satisfy.

2 – Sometimes our pain is related to personal sin. When you're hurting physically or emotionally, it's good to do a quick inventory to see if you have any unconfessed sin in your life. In Psalm 32:3-4, David links his physical pain and his emotional agony to his personal sin: "When I kept silent, my bones wasted away through my groaning all day long. For day and night your hand was heavy upon me; my strength was sapped as in the heat of summer." This theme is continued in Psalm 38:3, 17-18: "Because of your wrath there is no health in my body; my bones have no soundness because of my sin … For I am about to fall, and my pain is ever with me. I confess my iniquity; I am troubled by my sin." Personal sin may be a contributing factor to your illness and therefore should be taken seriously.

3 – Not all illness is directly linked to personal sin. We can certainly say that all illness ultimately is a result of Adam and Eve's sin, but we must be careful to not link every problem we have to some sin in our lives. This was the mistake that Job's friends made when they kept accusing him of wrongdoing. In their minds, Job was suffering because he had

somehow sinned. Let's be careful here. Some of you beat yourself up mercilessly as you blame yourself for your own pain. Others of you need to back off and stop giving your perspective on why someone else is suffering. Jesus addressed this prevalent mindset when he was asked to explain why a certain man was blind. His disciples wanted to know whether the man had sinned or his parents. Jesus answered in John 9:3: "Neither this man nor his parents sinned, but this happened so that the work of God might be displayed in his life."

4 – It's okay to go to professionals, but go to the Great Physician first. While there are some people who refuse to get any help because they want to trust God alone for their healing, it's my understanding that God often works His healing through doctors, other trained professionals, and through medicine. Remember that the bitter waters at Marah became better only when something was added to them. God could have made them sweet apart from any other means, but he chose to use the wood. Likewise God can heal with just a word from His mouth, but He uses other instruments as well. Having said that, what Asa did in the Old Testament is a warning to us. When he was sick, he didn't go to God first but instead went right to the doctor. This is described in 2 Chronicles 16:12: "Though his disease was severe, even in his illness he did not seek help from the LORD, but only from the physicians." Here's the point. Don't bypass the Great Physician on the way to the doctor's office.

5 – We need the community of faith. James 5:14-

16 describes what we should do when we are sick. First of all, call for the Elders of the church and ask for prayer. Second, confess your sins to others. Third, pray for each other. These steps are only possible if you're plugged into a community of faith. When you're hurting, you need the help of others. But sometimes those around us don't always know how to help. Be patient with others as God is patient with you.

6 – Faith is a force in healing. Some people mistakenly believe that if we just have enough faith, we can be healed of everything. At the other end of the spectrum, others think that God does not heal today and so they don't even pray about their problems. The proper biblical perspective is this. Pray earnestly for healing to Jehovah Rapha, and have faith to believe that He can heal you, but be careful about demanding that He answer your prayers according to your will. We are to pray according to His will. Tim Hansel writes: "I have prayed hundreds, if not thousands of times for the Lord to heal me…and He finally healed me of the need to be healed."

Having said that, we need to keep Mark 6:5-6 in mind. This passage explains the importance of faith to Jesus: "He could not do any miracles there, except lay his hands on a few sick people and heal them. And he was amazed at their lack of faith." Faith somehow unleashes the healing power of God. James 4:2 says, "You do not have, because you do not ask God."

7 – Some healing takes place in unusual ways.

There is a story about a pastor who was in a church and was asked to pray for a man who had cancer. He prayed boldly for the man's healing and that next week the pastor received a telephone call from the man's wife. She said, "You prayed for my husband. He had cancer." The pastor thought when he heard her use the past tense that his cancer had been eradicated.

But then she said, "He died." He felt terrible. But she continued, "Don't feel bad. When you saw him he was filled with anger. He knew he was going to be dead in a short period of time, and he hated God. He was 58 years old, and he wanted to see his children and grandchildren grow up. He was angry that this all powerful God didn't take away his sickness and heal him. He would lie in bed and curse God. The more his anger grew towards God, the more miserable he was to everybody around him. It was an awful thing to be in his presence."

But the lady told the pastor, "After you prayed for him, a peace had come over him and a joy had come into him. The last three days have been the best days of our lives. We've sung. We've laughed. We've read Scripture. We prayed. Oh, they've been wonderful days. And I called to thank you for laying your hands on him and praying for healing." And then she said something incredibly profound.

"He wasn't cured, but he was healed."

8 – Don't be careless about communion. My sense is that we don't think enough about the seriousness of this ordinance. In 1 Corinthians 11:29-30, Paul tells Christians to approach the elements

with a sense of awe and to make sure we are living in unity with others. If we don't, we're in danger of actually becoming sick or even dying: "For anyone who eats and drinks without recognizing the body of the Lord eats and drinks judgment on himself. That is why many among you are weak and sick, and a number of you have fallen asleep."

9 – The Cross of Christ is the source of healing. The Jehovah who heals in the Old Testament is the Jesus who heals in the New. Don't miss the significance behind the wood from a tree providing sweetness to the bitter water. All of our problems began at a tree in the Garden of Eden and our sin problem is resolved because another piece of wood was used to hold up our sin substitute on the cross. Isaiah 53:5 says that "the punishment that brought us peace was upon him, and by his wounds we are healed." 1 Peter 2:24 picks up on this prophecy: "He himself bore our sins in his body on the tree, so that we might die to sins and live for righteousness; by his wounds you have been healed." Only Jesus can sweeten the bitterness of life. He is the bondage breaker. As Leviticus 26:13 says: "I broke the bars of your yoke and enabled you to walk with heads held high."

Maybe you've fallen recently and it feels like you've crashed so quickly you don't even know what happened. Whether you're hurting emotionally, physically or spiritually, turn to Jehovah Rapha right now. Let's think about Exodus 15 again for a moment. After God made the sour waters sweet, He then led the Israelites to a place called Elim. We read in verse 27 that Elim had twelve springs and seventy palm trees. God led them to a place of plenty. Even if we're not cured we can be healed by Jesus. He is both the wood and the living water as He said in John 7:37: "If anyone is thirsty, let him come to me and drink." The only way to go from Marah to Elim is to turn to Jesus, who is Jehovah Rapha.

A CONSUMING FIRE

Hebrews 12:29 says, "For our God is a consuming fire." What exactly does that mean? Most of us are aware of the story of Sodom and Gomorrah, two cities whose people were so sinful that angels were sent to warn Lot to abandon the city with his family before it was destroyed.

"Then the Lord rained upon Sodom and upon Gomorrah brimstone and fire from the Lord out of heaven; And he overthrew those cities, and all the plain, and all the inhabitants of the cities, and that which grew upon the ground." (Genesis 19:24-25) No doubt the writer of Hebrews was well aware of that story.

Again, many of us are familiar with the story of the prophet Elijah and his contest with the 800 prophets of Baal on Mount Carmel. It seems the people of Israel could not decide which God to follow: Jehovah Almighty, the God of Abraham, Isaac, and Jacob, or Baal. To settle the dispute, each side was to build an altar and place a sacrifice on it for their god to consume.

The prophets of Baal went first with dancing and praying, even cutting themselves and crying out all morning for their god to receive the bull sacrifice, all to no avail. Then Elijah built his altar and placed the bull sacrifice on it, and just for good measure, had a trench dug around it and had it filled with water. He even had the wood and meat saturated with water.

Then Elijah prayed to the Lord and asked Him to receive the sacrifice so the people might see that He was the Lord and the only true God. 1 Kings 18:38 tells us, "Then the fire of the Lord fell and burned up the sacrifice, the wood, the stones and the soil, and also licked up the water in the trench."

The people of Israel got a first-hand look at the meaning of Hebrews 12:29. Yet this explanation of God does not end in the Old Testament. I am certain we have all been taught, or at least heard, of Hell and the fires of Hell and how it all goes down in the end. John makes things perfectly clear in the Book of Revelation.

"The sea gave up the dead that were in it, and death and Hades gave up the dead that were in them, and each person was judged according to what they had done. Then death and Hades were thrown into the lake of fire. The lake of fire is the second death. Anyone whose name was not found written in the book of life was thrown into the lake of fire." (Revelation 20:13-15)

I hope you are beginning to see, at least on the surface, how God is a consuming fire and my hope is that we don't take that lightly. When you begin to realize that fire literally does come from God, you realize that you can be consumed to death.

There are other elements to this consuming fire as well. Take the story of Moses on Mount Horeb, when he saw the burning bush and heard the call of God.

"And the angel of the Lord appeared unto him in a flame of fire out of the midst of a bush: and he looked, and, behold, the bush burned with fire, and the bush was not consumed." (Exodus 3:2)

This time death and destruction are not the result of the consuming fire, but insight and revelation. The same seems true of Isaiah when he had his vision in the temple after the death of King Uzziah in Isaiah chapter 6. In his vision, Isaiah sees the Lord sitting on a throne high and lifted up and angels appear, declaring holiness to God, the temple shakes and fills with smoke and Isaiah is struck down with fear and awe. An angel takes from the altar a burning coal held in tongs and touches the mouth of Isaiah saying: "... your guilt is taken away and your sin forgiven ..."

Like the fire in the burning bush, this fiery coal brings the revelation of God, healing, and then a call to serve. The prophet Malachi calls this element of God the refiner's fire.

"But who can endure the day of his coming? Who can stand when he appears? For he will be like a refiner's fire or a launderer's soap. He will sit as a refiner and purifier of silver; he will purify the Levites and refine them like gold and silver. Then the Lord will have men who will bring offerings in righteousness, " (Malachi 3:2)

The fire of God here is a source to purify and make holy, like diamonds that need dirt and grime chipped off and the rough edges worn down, that we may shine brilliantly as intended. God is not merely in the destruction business—wiping out cities and destroying evil people—but there is something else to His consuming fire and that is the power to refine us and make us new creations in Christ Jesus.

John who is so explicit in talking about God's wrath and judgment in the book of Revelation is just as explicit in describing to us the image of the risen

Christ whose eyes were like a flame of fire (Rev.1:14) and when seeing the risen Christ, like Moses and Isaiah, fell to the ground overcome with fear and trembling, humbled to the point of nothingness before the Lord God, but told to rise up and to write the revelation he was given.

Insight, cleansing, serving.

This element of refining and purifying, a part of the consuming fire of God, is one that many of us are not so sure we want to deal with because the transforming power of God in our lives can be scary and demanding—even painful—calling us to change when we don't want to and to move out of the comfort zone we have made for our self, or giving up the sin we continue to find temporary pleasure in. We have only to look again at Moses to see that he was not necessarily a willing candidate for divine refining and purifying. He had all kinds of excuses to hinder God's work in and for him.

All we have to do is look at our priorities and see where we spend the most time and money to realize how much we are like Moses in our resistance to God's shaping our lives; still He remains whether we like it or not—a consuming fire capable of death and destruction but wanting to refine and purify those He has called and chosen.

There is one other element I cannot fail to mention and that is the reward, the blessing when you and I are willing to respond obediently to the refiner's work in and through us. It happened with Moses, when he finally stopped questioning and challenging God and got with the program. Moses went to Pharaoh and told him to let the Israelite slaves go.

And God worked in only ways that He can work and the Israelites were released. On the way out of Egypt and heading toward the promised land, this point is made in the Scriptures:

"By day the Lord went ahead of them in a pillar of cloud to guide them on their way and by night in a pillar of fire to give them light, so that they could travel by day or night." (Exodus 13:21)

God displayed his blessing and protection over his people in the form of a cloud as a shade protecting them from the burning sun, and fire to light the way in the darkness of night. There is so much more that could be said about this fire for the Israelites, but certainly we can see that blessing and reward comes to those who will trust and obey.

One final example of this blessing that comes through the fire of God is seen at Pentecost. The disciples were gathered in an upper room in Jerusalem waiting for the Holy Spirit as Christ had instructed them. It is recorded in Acts 2:

"And suddenly a sound came from Heaven like the rush of a mighty wind, and it filled all the house where they were sitting. And there appeared to them tongues as of fire, distributed and resting on each of the disciples. And they were all filled with the Holy Spirit and began to speak in other tongues as the Spirit enabled them." (Acts 2:2-4)

Like the pillar of fire that went before the Israelites, the fire of God in the form of tongues was not destroying or purifying as much as being a source of blessing and divine reward that ushers in a gift as each disciple began to speak in other tongues as the Spirit gave them the ability.

I have not come close to exhausting the meaning or explanation of the Hebrews writer's words—*for our God is a consuming fire*—but enough I hope to awaken us to the point that these are not simply symbolic nor empty words to be glossed over as we read them. Rather these words remind us anew of the awesome wrath and judgment of God as well as His earnest desire to refine us into His glorified creation that shares in His blessing and rewards.

WRATHFUL

Most Christians find the wrath of God difficult to understand or believe. The idea of a wrathful God has been for some Christians a roadblock to faith. There are those of us who have experienced the transforming grace and love of Jesus in our lives and find the thought of God's wrath to be a contradiction of our experience. Is it possible that the God whose unconditional love is revealed in Paul's statement "that, while we were yet sinners, Christ died for us" is at the same time a God of wrath?

The Bible speaks about God's nature, work, and purposes in terms we understand and have experienced. While this is necessary, we need to remember the human mind can never fully comprehend the absolute nature of God. We see God as One who is or possesses truth, grace, beauty, love, righteousness, and faithfulness in their most complete or absolute forms. We do not see this in humans. While we do see forms of these in humans, we also see hate, anger, a vindictive spirit, ugliness and wrath.

What we see in God we perceive to be positive and we long to possess these attributes. What we see in ourselves and others we perceive to be negative and our desire is to rid ourselves and our nation of these negative aspects.

The reason we find it very difficult to apply negative human aspects to God is an idealistic, romantic idea of God that has its foundation in philosophical speculation. This is not the biblical idea of God. In the Bible both God and the world is viewed more seriously than abstract philosophical speculation.

We are told in the Bible that God enters into a relationship with His creation in Jesus of Nazareth, in whom "all the fullness of God was pleased to dwell" (Colossians 1:19), who at the same is "in all respects like us" (Hebrews 2:17). The Bible also takes the relationship between Creator and creature more seriously than we do.

Since the creation is God's, it is responsible to God. Here is where we have a difficult time accepting. We want to do our own thing and when our own thing brings us down, we want to play the blame game even though the Bible clearly teaches, we reap what we sow.

The foundation of Paul's doctrine on the wrath of God is found in Genesis chapter three, especially verses 21-22. In the Genesis account of creation the refusal of mankind to live as creature in the Creator-creature relationship is summed up in Romans 1:25.

Paul speaks of the wrath of God in two ways; the first is a future event in which God's judgments will be executed on the world's sinfulness (Romans 2:5). Where he tells the Romans, and all who read his letter to the Romans, "because of your stubbornness and unrepentant heart you are storing up wrath for yourself in the day of wrath and revelation of the righteous judgment of God" Paul sees God's wrath and judgment as an activity of God, His decided action against sin, but not against the sinner. The sinner becomes involved in the wrath of God and the righteous judgment of God because he is involved in sin. Paul is telling the Romans God's personal response to sin is not like the response of their various gods. His response is never characterized by or given to willful and often unwise or irrational choices and demands, vindictiveness or malice.

The second is where Paul also tells his readers, "God's wrath is being revealed from heaven now." God's wrath is not only a response to man's unfaithfulness in the future judgment; it is already present. We see it every day. It is reported in news broadcasts. In our newspapers. And we ask ourselves what is happening. God is sending us wake-up calls and we are simply shutting off the alarm.

The human condition Paul describes in Romans 1:18-32 is not something caused by God, but the sinfulness of mankind and its results when God's will is violated. God's wrath is revealed in the fact that mankind has rejected God's truth, the truth about God's nature and will. When the truth about God's nature and His will is rejected the result is futile thinking, idolatry, perversion of God-intended sexuality, and relational-moral brokenness.

A prime example is the state of our land today.

The sinful perversion of human existence is the result of human decisions and should be understood as God's punishment which we bring upon ourselves. It is our will in conflict with God's will.

The idea God punishes or blesses in direct proportion to our sinful or good deeds cannot be Biblically supported. God's unconditional love has been demonstrated in that, while we were sinners,

Christ died for us. His love is everlasting. The rejection of that love separates us from its life-giving power.

The Bible declares God's love for us repeatedly.

1 John 4:19: "We love because he first loved us."
1 Peter 5:7: "Cast all your anxiety on him because he cares for you."

And of course, everyone's favorite verse, "For God so loved the world, that he gave his one and only Son, that whoever believes in him shall not perish but have eternal life." (John 3:16)

During His ministry on earth, Jesus told a parable about how much God loved us. He told about a young man who demanded his inheritance and then—without so much as a goodbye he "…set off for a distant country and there squandered his wealth in wild living." (Luke 15:13)

As long as he had money, he lived the high life and had all kinds of friends. But once the money was gone… so were his friends. Then, when all his money was gone, a famine struck the land, and without money or friends this boy had to find a job. But the only job he could find was working for a pig farmer; one of the lowest forms of life a Jew could imagine.

At one point, he gets so hungry that he looks at the slop the pigs are eating and starts to wonder if it would be something even he could eat. It was at this point he finally realizes what a mess he's made of his life. And it occurs to him that even his dad's servants were eating better than he was. So, he made a plan.

He would go back to his father and say: "Father, I have sinned against heaven and against you. I am no longer worthy to be called your son; make me like one of your hired men."

The Pharisees would probably have told this story with a different ending. When the son came back and told the father he wasn't worthy to be called his son... the dad agreed. "Yes, you aren't worthy to be called my son. So you'll work as a servant for a few years to prove your repentance. Then maybe I'll let you be my son again."

But that wasn't how Jesus told the story, because Jesus was teaching us how much God loved us. "... while he was still a long way off, his father saw him and was filled with compassion for him; he ran to his son, threw his arms around him and kissed him...

(And he) said to his servants, 'Quick! Bring the best robe and put it on him. Put a ring on his finger and sandals on his feet. Bring the fattened calf and kill it. Let's have a feast and celebrate. For this son of mine was dead and is alive again; he was lost and is found.' So they began to celebrate." (Luke 15:20, 22-24)

That's our God. The God of Scripture that Jesus came to tell us about. The God of love and compassion who cares for us.

But.

We also read passages about a God who "hates."

Proverbs 6:16-19 says, "There are six things the LORD hates, seven that are detestable to him: haughty eyes, a lying tongue, hands that shed innocent blood, a heart that devises wicked schemes, feet that are quick to rush into evil, a false witness who pours out lies and a man who stirs up dissension among brothers."

The Bible tells us God hates a number of things and people. So how do we reconcile a loving God with a God who hates? There are some who have tried to explain that there are two gods in Scripture. There are some people who believe that there's a God of the Old Testament and a God of the New Testament. A God known for judgment and wrath. And then they believe that there is a God of the New Testament who is loving and compassionate. They believe in two separate and distinct gods.

The Bible has a word for this. It's called heresy. You could also call it false doctrine. Or you could simply call it dumb, because that idea is not taught in Scripture anywhere.

So here's the deal. God hates evil. And God hates those who practice evil.

Proverbs 3:32: "…The LORD detests a perverse man."

Psalm 5:5: "The arrogant cannot stand in your presence; you hate all who do wrong."

Psalm 11:5: "The LORD examines the righteous, but the wicked and those who love violence his soul hates."

I am sure you recall that Jesus wasn't real keen on some people:

"Woe to you, teachers of the law and Pharisees, you hypocrites! You are like whitewashed tombs, which look beautiful on the outside but on the inside are full of dead men's bones and everything unclean." (Matthew 23:27)

Those are hateful words from Jesus—focused on a hateful group of men.

Does that seem right? That God would hate people? I mean, isn't there a proverb of some kind that says "God hates sin…" and what's the rest of it? Oh yeah "but He loves the sinner."

Apparently, that's not *entirely* true. God does hate certain people—perverse men, all those who do wrong, the wicked, and those who love violence.

But why?

Why would God hate these people?

Because these people do hateful things.

Their eyes are haughty. They're proud and arrogant people.

They have lying tongues. They deceive people to take advantage of them.

Their hands shed innocent blood. Whether it's the hate-filled bombers who killed and maimed so many people at the Boston Marathon, or the money-hungry

Planned Parenthood and its abortion doctors who destroy the lives of unborn children. Life means nothing to these people.

Their hearts devise wicked schemes. One of the most powerful condemnations of the people who died in Noah's flood was this: "The LORD saw that the wickedness of man was great in the earth, and that every intention of the thoughts of his heart was only evil continually." (Genesis 6:5)

Their feet are quick to rush to evil. They can't wait to do bad things. They hurt others out of the pure joy of doing it.

They are false witnesses who pour out lies. They gossip about others. They say mean and hateful things, all with the intention of dragging others down around them.

And they stir up dissension among brothers. One of the terms you might hear used is people create "drama". They deliberately stir up trouble between people so that they can sit back and watch. It's like they can't get away to watch their favorite soap operas, so they create their own dramas wherever they are.

God hates all that. And he hates those who do it. There are two reasons God hates this. Firstly, because they have hated him first. "I, the LORD your God, am a jealous God, punishing the children for the sin of the fathers to the third and fourth generation of those who hate me." (Exodus 20:5)

God holds certain people in contempt because of the contempt those people have held against the things God called holy, and so they literally hated

God first. Secondly, God hates these people because of what they have done to other people.

Notice that every sin listed in Proverbs 6 is an action taken against other people.

The haughty eyes: they're looking down on others.

Lying tongues: they're lying to people.

Hands that shed innocent blood: they kill people.

Hearts that devise wicked schemes: they plot to hurt others.

Feet rushing to do evil: they can't wait to hurt others.

False witness: saying false things against other people.

And stirring up dissension "drama" among their brothers.

Each and every sin listed in this passage tells of wicked people who hurt others. Others who are made in the image of God. Imagine someone hurting someone in your family who you love. Doing mean and painful things that damage that person. Wouldn't you get angry and wouldn't you feel a bit of hatred for someone who would be so mean and cruel to your loved one?

Of course you would. You would take it personal.

And God takes it personal. He hates it.

A. W. Tozer described it this way: "God's wrath is His utter intolerance of whatever degrades and destroys. He hates iniquity as a mother hated the polio that would take the life of the child."

If my child were caught in the grips of a deadly disease, you better believe I'd hate that disease. And you better believe I'd do everything I could to fight that disease. And you better believe I'd do whatever I could to destroy that disease.

Why? Because it hurt someone I love.

And that's how God hates sin. God hates sin because he hates the damage and death it brings to those He loves.

All too often, we see people at demonstrations holding up signs that say things like:

"God hates America."

"God hates Planned Parenthood."

"God hates Queers."

And they look like they are happy that God hates these people. But there is something seriously wrong with that kind of thinking. And what's wrong is this: many people think of sinners as being the "other people." It's those people who are sinners, not me. I'm a nice person, just ask me. But the Bible says we have all sinned. Ephesians 2:3 says, "All of us also lived among them at one time, gratifying the cravings of our sinful nature and following its desires and thoughts. Like the rest, we were by nature objects of wrath."

You and I have all done hateful things.

Paul also had this to say to the people of Galatia:

"The acts of the sinful nature are obvious: sexual immorality, impurity and debauchery; idolatry and witchcraft; hatred, discord, jealousy, fits of rage, selfish ambition, dissensions, factions and envy;

drunkenness, orgies, and the like. I warn you, as I did before, that those who live like this will not inherit the kingdom of God." (Galatians 5:19-21)

Paul warned them, again, that people who live like this will not inherit the kingdom of God. And he wasn't talking to those "other people", he was talking to the Christians that were in Galatia. That's right, Christians. And he was warning them that there was a danger in living that way, the danger being that they would not inherit the kingdom. In other words, they would end up in hell.

This is a story from a pastor friend of mine. Years ago a young man started coming to church after he'd been devastated by a divorce. His wife had left him and his two sons and he was looking for God's help. After a few weeks he realized his need to have Jesus in his life and he was baptized into Christ.

He was faithful in church for several months, but then he stopped coming. Then it was found out that he had a live-in girlfriend and the pastor went out to his home to investigate.

He confirmed that he was living with the woman and that he had no intention of marrying her. He'd been burned in marriage and didn't want it to happen again. But he loved this woman and especially appreciated how she showed love to his two young sons.

It was explained that this was wrong. That God condemned this kind of lifestyle and that it could cost him his salvation.

But he said he didn't care – this woman cared for him and his sons. He said, "I don't care what happens to me, as long as my sons are taken care of."

It was then the pastor pointed to Exodus 20:5 "I, the LORD your God, am a jealous God, punishing the children for the sin of the fathers to the third and fourth generation of those who hate me."

It was explained that his actions would hurt not only him—but his children and his children's children. His sin was going to damage the very children he said he cared about and wanted to protect. He failed to understand the danger he was putting both himself and his children in.

And that's where the good news comes in. God doesn't want that. God does hate the sin and the sinner, but that does not mean he likes that arrangement. In fact, in Exodus 20 it not only says that if we hate God, God will punish us by "visiting the iniquity of the fathers on the children to the third and the fourth generation of those who hate me **but** showing steadfast love to thousands of those who love me and keep my commandments." (Exodus 20:5-6)

What God is saying is this: If you do evil things – there is a price to be paid. He will bring punishment upon you and your children and your children's children.

But.

If you decide that you don't want that future for your family. If you decide that you've been foolish to do hurtful things to God. If you decide you want to turn around, repent, and stop living for yourself and start living for God and pleasing Him then He'll break the cycle of destruction in your life. Before you repented, you would just be bringing heartache on your family, but after you repented God would break the cycle of that curse and bring blessings upon thousands of those who loved him and kept His commandments.

How would God do that? How could God undo all the damage of bad decisions?

Ephesians says: "All of us also lived among them at one time, gratifying the cravings of our sinful nature and following its desires and thoughts. Like the rest, we were by nature objects of wrath. But because of his great love for us, God, who is rich in mercy, made us alive with Christ even when we were dead in transgressions—it is by grace you have been saved." (Ephesians 2:3-5)

You were dead in your transgressions.

You were by nature objects of wrath.

You had nothing to offer God.

But because of His great love and mercy God made us alive with Jesus. Not because of your righteousness, but because of Christ's.

LIFE

Jesus gave his mission statement in a very clear way in the book of John. John 10:10 says:

"The enemy comes to steal, kill, and destroy; I have come that you may have life, and have it to the full."

In order to understand the life that Jesus intended for us, we must first understand the enemy and his intent.

Who is the enemy?

Ephesians 6:12 says: "For our struggle is not against flesh and blood, but against the rulers, against the authorities, against the powers of this dark world and against the spiritual forces of evil in the heavenly realms."

Our battle is **not** against other *people*. We do not struggle against flesh and blood, but against the rulers and authorities of spiritual forces. We tend to focus our attention on abortionists, godless politicians, pornographers, drug dealers, and other purveyors of filth. But these people are only the unwitting pawns of the real enemy. They are morally culpable for their choices, but they are in the service of evil beings who influence them in ways they don't even realize.

Sometimes we even make it more personal,

especially when someone has hurt us. "That person is the source of my problems." Yet our struggle is not against flesh and blood though it may seem that way much of the time.

The other thing this verse reveals is that there are various kinds of demonic powers. There are *rulers*, *authorities*, *powers of this dark world*, and *spiritual forces of evil in the heavenly realms*. It is not clear how we should differentiate between them, but perhaps it is enough to know that just as there are different types of angels, so too are there different types of demons. And we are all foot soldiers in a vast invisible war that stretches across the cosmos.

Where did he come from?

"Son of man, take up a lament concerning the king of Tyre and say to him: 'This is what the Sovereign LORD says:

"You seal the measure, full of wisdom and perfect in beauty. You have been in Eden, the garden of God; every precious stone was your covering, the ruby, the topaz, and the diamond, the beryl, the onyx, and the jasper, the sapphire, the turquoise, and the emerald, and gold. The workmanship of your tabrets and of your pipes in you - in the day you were created, they were prepared. You were the guardian cherub that covers, and I had put you in the holy height of God, where you were. You walked up and down in the midst of the stones of fire. You were perfect in your ways from the day you were created, until iniquity was found in you. By the multitude of your trade they filled your midst with violence, and you sinned. So I cast you profaned from the height of God, and I destroyed you, O covering cherub, from among the stones of fire. Your heart was lifted up because of your beauty; you corrupted your wisdom because of your splendor. I have cast you to the ground. I will put you before kings, that they may see you. By the host of your iniquities, by the iniquity of your trade, you have profaned your holy places; thus I brought a fire from your midst; it shall devour you, and I will give you for ashes on the earth, in the sight of all who see you. All who know you among the peoples shall be appalled at you; you shall be terrors, and you will not be forever." (Ezekiel 28:12-19)

Those verses give us insight into where Satan came from. This verse is talking about the literal king of Tyrus, but it also refers to Satan. God made Satan to be full of wisdom and perfect in beauty. God covered him with every precious stone. The stones listed are actually the same as the ones used on the high priests' apparel with the exception of three.

The gold is specifically representative of kingly apparel. The Mercy Seat in the temple was made of pure gold. The idea of "workmanship" indicates that Satan was made for a specific service. Satan had tabrets (timbrels) and pipes (flute or horn) built into his body. The idea of "prepared" indicates these were designed by God with a specific purpose. Satan was to use these to lead the heavenly hosts in worship to God. God designed music for the purpose of worship, and Satan was Heaven's worship leader.

Satan was the anointed cherub that covered. The concept of "anointed" means to be set apart for service to God. God said that Satan was upon the holy mountain of God. This was the place set apart or exalted for God. Satan was in the presence of God walking up and down in the middle of the stones of fire. What an amazing sight!

Satan was perfect in his ways, his thoughts, and his actions from the time God created him. Then iniquity was found in him. The word iniquity means perverseness. God bluntly says that Satan sinned. Notice God's words: "So I cast you profaned from the height of God." God is in control.

Satan began to look at his beauty and focus his attention on himself. Once he had seen from God's perspective (true wisdom), but then that wisdom became darkened as he looked at himself.

"How you have fallen from heaven, morning star, son of the dawn! You have been cast down to the earth, you who once laid low the nations! You said in your heart, "I will ascend to the heavens; I will raise my throne above the stars of God; I will sit enthroned on the mount of assembly, on the utmost heights of Mount Zaphon. I will ascend above the tops of the clouds; I will make myself like the Most High." (Isaiah 14:12-14)

Lucifer is the original name given to the devil. The name Lucifer means "shining one." That is interesting because we see that God created Lucifer to reflect God's glory. Now, however, he only appears as an angel of light, when he really is an angel of darkness.

What does he do?

Steal

I once saw a prank video of a man who dressed himself up to look like an elderly person. He then went into various convenient stores and attempted to "shoplift" candy.

In the spiritual realm, a kind of stealing is going on in many lives that is very serious. Satan is in the business of ripping off things far more important than candy from the checkout line. That is his nature.

Satan obviously doesn't want candy. Or your house. Or your vehicle, your clothes, or your money. But he is very interested in stealing spiritual treasures—things that are of value with God and are of eternal significance. Take, for example, our very purpose for living. Satan loves snatching men and women on the streets of my city—and your city—people who have potential and turning them into glassy-eyed wanderers through life, with no goal from day to day.

They lie in bed at night staring at the ceiling, saying: "What's the point? Just to make money? Just to have kids? Why?"

People turn to drugs and alcohol because they don't have a clue as to why they are alive. Others turn to career achievement, or pleasure, of stuff ... something, anything to fill the void. But it doesn't work. God created us to worship and enjoy Him forever, but this knowledge has been stolen from their awareness. Notice the progression in John 10:10. Satan's first move is petty larceny, then on to killing, and then to mass destruction. But it all starts with stealing.

Even among those of us who are Christians, the devil has a strategy of theft. The tragic loss of our "first love" for Jesus. There was a time in our lives when we loved Jesus so much more than we do today. We longed for God's Word. Our love for God's house was enthusiastic. Our eagerness for spreading the gospel was so strong … Now, how is it? Yes, we still love the Lord. We still come to church. But what happened to all that energy and passion?

That is the problem Jesus addressed with the Ephesian church in Revelation 2:2-5: "I know your deeds, your hard work and your perseverance… Yet I hold this against you: You have forsaken your first love. Remember the height from which you have fallen! Repent and do the things you did at first. If you do not repent, I will come to you and remove your lamp stand from its place."

Where does our "first love" go? Our zeal and our intensity don't evaporate. Satan steals the hot embers of devotion and consecration. We get ripped off.

Someone might say, "Well, you have to understand that back when I met Christ, I was an energetic teenager. A lot has happened since then. You know, we all mellow out with time." Does anyone really believe that?

The Bible says God's plan for us is that we be "transformed into his likeness with ever-increasing glory, which comes from the Lord, who is the Spirit" (2 Corinthians 3:18). There is no end to the power he wants to exhibit in our lives. The Bible has no retirement plan. God can keep his people on fire for Him; can keep them sharp and intense. We need to be honest and admit what has really happened. There is no point in conning ourselves. We've been ripped off by the master thief.

Or how about that unique calling that rests on every Christian's life, the desire to serve others in the name of the Lord? Five years ago there was a stirring inside of you; He gave you a dream about what He wanted to do in your life. Maybe He wanted you to teach children. Maybe he wanted you to be a prayer warrior, standing in the gap for other people in need. Maybe there was even a pull toward the mission field that was birthed by the Holy Spirit himself. But then... you got discouraged. Somebody let you down. Something went sour at your church. You tried once or twice, but somebody criticized you. Soon the dream was gone, and the calling wasn't so real. All the inspiration you had felt was missing.

Where do you think they all went? Something very precious was stolen along the way. The devil is always trying to rob us of something God blessed us with. When he succeeds, the spiritual gifts seem to fade, and the material things occupy our attention twenty-four hours a day.

Consider the subject of marriage. Did you know that the divorce rate among churchgoers is just about equal with the population at large? If I were an atheist or an agnostic, I'd say, "Look, how come Jesus can't keep you two together? I thought you said he was so wonderful?"

Why are Christian couples breaking up? Is it because they shouldn't have gotten married in the first place? Or because they came from dysfunctional homes and had bad role models? There is more to it than that. The thief comes to steal.

The fact is that Satan fully intends to destroy our

marriages. These are the realities of spiritual warfare. Only the power of Christ can keep two imperfect people together as God has planned and can give them victory over Satan's destructive power. We do battle against the forces set on stealing our marriages, credibility, and effectiveness.

What about our children and our grandchildren? They were dedicated to God at one time. But something has happened in the years since then. Now the young man or young woman is not living for God, and there's no use pretending that they are. Let's not close our eyes and make-believe otherwise. Before we can see God do what only he can do, we must really see what is going on around us.

The enemy comes to steal, kill, and destroy. Some translations use the word thief instead of enemy. The word thief comes from the Greek word *klepto*, which means to steal. It gives a picture of a bandit, pickpocket, or thief who is so artful in the way he steals that his exploits of thievery are nearly undetectable. This reminds me of pickpockets in Las Vegas. They can slip their hands into a person's pockets, take what they want, and be long gone before that person ever discovers they were there.

Jesus uses this word to let us know how extremely cunning the devil is in the way that he steals from people. He knows that if he does it outright, his actions will be recognized; therefore, he steals from people in such a deceptive way that he often accomplishes his evil goal before they know they have been stolen from.

Often the devil injects thoughts into a person's mind to steal their peace, their joy, and even their beliefs. The word *klepto* describes a thief's uncontrollable urge to get his hands into someone's pockets so he can take that which doesn't rightfully belong to him. It's interesting that this is where we get the word kleptomaniac, which describes a person with a persistent, neurotic impulse to steal. Just as a kleptomaniac can't help but steal, the devil can't stop stealing because it is his impulse and his very nature to steal. This is precisely the nature and behavior of the thief Jesus told us about.

In the middle of all these losses is the silent theft of the most crucial element in our spiritual walk: our faith.

What is faith? It is total dependence upon God. People with faith develop a second kind of sight. They see more than just the circumstances; they see God, right beside them. Can they prove it? No. But by faith they know he's there nonetheless. Without faith, says Hebrews 11:6, it's impossible to please God. Nothing else counts if faith is missing. There is no other foundation for Christian living, no matter the amount of self-effort or energy spent. Nothing else touches the Father's heart as much as when his children simply trust Him. I meet people who at one time would pray over anything and everything! Even if they lost their keys, they would pray to find them—and amazingly, the keys would show up. Now the same people seem not to believe that God can do much of anything. They will still give the standard confession of faith: "Yes, I have faith in the God who answers prayer." But that vibrant trust and expectation are gone. They aren't saying, "Come on, let's go after this problem in the name of the Lord."

They've been *robbed*.

Kill

Not only does the enemy come to steal, but Jesus also said that he comes "to kill." At first glance, it appears that he means to kill, as to take someone's life. However, the Greek word is *thuo*, which means to sacrifice. It originally referred to the sacrificial giving of animals on the altar. It could mean to sacrifice, to surrender, or to give up something that is precious and dear. It was particularly used in a religious connotation to denote the sacrifice of animals and it had nothing to do with killing in terms of murder.

Because Jesus uses this word to describe the work of the thief in John 10:10, he is telling us that if the thief hasn't already walked away with everything we hold precious and dear, he will then try to convince us that we need to sacrifice everything he hasn't already taken from us.

The thief cannot bear the fact that you possess any kind of blessing. Therefore, if he is unsuccessful at stealing the good things from your life, he will try to cunningly convince you to give up everything you possess and love—simply because he doesn't want you to have it. He may even try to create stressful situations that cause you to conclude that your only solution is to sacrifice the things you love.

Destroy

Then Jesus went on to say that the thief also comes "to destroy." The word destroy is from the Greek word *apolummi*, meaning to destroy. *Apolummi* is essentially three words. *Apo*, which means away from or wholly plus *olethros*, which means state of utter ruin. *Allumi* means destroy; from the root *apollyon* (destroyer). It means to destroy utterly but not ceasing to exist. It is to be so completely ruined that you can no longer serve the purpose for which you were created.

If the enemy cannot successfully steal from you or get you to sacrifice what you hold dear, he will try to ruin it.

An expanded interpretive translation of John 10:10 could be:

"The thief wants to get his hands into every good thing in your life. In fact, this pickpocket is looking for any opportunity to wiggle his way so deep into your personal affairs that he can walk off with everything you hold precious and dear. And that's not all—when he's finished stealing all your goods and possessions, he'll take his plan to rob you blind to the next level. He'll create conditions so horrible that you will see no way to solve the problem except to sacrifice everything that remains from his previous attacks. The goal of this thief is to totally waste and devastate your life. You will end up feeling as if you are finished and out of business. Make no mistake, the enemy's ultimate aim is to obliterate you."

Life

But Jesus went on to say, "I have come that they may have life, and have it to the fullest." The words "they might have" are from the Greek tense that means to have and to continually possess. The life Jesus offers us is *zoe*, which suggests a life that is filled with vitality. The word abundantly is from the Greek word *periossos*, and it means above, beyond what is regular, extraordinary, or even exceeding. This is not just abundance, it is super abundance.

What a comparison! The devil comes to steal, kill, and destroy, but Jesus has come to give us life as we have never known it.

An expanded interpretive translation of the second half of this verse could be:

"But I have come that they may have, keep, and constantly retain a vitality, gusto, vigor, and zest for living that springs up from deep down inside. I came that they might embrace this unrivaled, unequaled, matchless, incomparable, richly loaded and overflowing life to the ultimate maximum."

There is an obscure story at the end of 1 Samuel that speaks to this matter in vivid detail. It is one of the low points on the roller coaster of David's life. The young conqueror of the giant Goliath is now on the run from King Saul. So many threats, so many close calls. He actually goes to live among the Philistines for a year, because he has run out of places to hide in Israel. David has his own little militia of six hundred men, plus wives and children. They set up at a place called Ziklag. When the Philistines decide to go to war against Israel, it puts David in a real crunch. He's a fighter, of course, a warrior, so he lines up with King Achish. But the Philistine generals spot him and say to their king, "What does David think he's doing?"

"Why? What do you mean?"

The generals say, "Look, don't you know that song they sang all over Israel? 'Saul has slain his thousands, and David his tens of thousands'-and some of those tens of thousands were us! He is definitely not going into battle with us."

So David and his militia get sent back home. When they come close to Ziklag, they start to see smoke on the horizon. They run home and soon discover something dreadful: Every wife, every son, every daughter, every cow and lamb is gone. Someone has made a secret raid, burning down the city and stealing everything. These husbands and fathers are stunned and heartbroken. Imagine them thinking of their wives and daughters being captured by some roving band of marauders. My lovely wife is missing! What is happening to my fourteen-year-old daughter right now? They can only imagine the brutality and heartlessness that have surely occurred. They begin to cry so hard that they run out of tears. They are devastated.

David's family is gone, too. Everything is *lost*.

At such a moment of human sorrow, other emotions come into play. Anger and resentment boil up. David's men begin saying, "What were we doing out there, anyway? Whose bright idea was it to go join the Philistine army? We should have been taking care of our families. Let's stone David for this!" Then comes this wonderful phrase in 1 Samuel 30:6: "But David found strength in the LORD his God." As the bottom was falling out of his life, he went to a quiet place to pray and gather himself before God. Having gotten back his poise, his spiritual equilibrium, David goes for a consultation with God about what he should do. Whenever David was walking in grace, he never just shot from the hip; he first sought the Lord.

"Should I chase those who destroyed our town, and if I do, will I find them?" he asks.

God replies, "Yes, go after them—and you will find them."

So they take off. Along the way, riding across the desert, they come upon a half-conscious Egyptian slave. After they revive him with some cool water, the man admits some vital information. "I was with the Amalekites, and we raided the area, but then I got sick."

"Well, how would you like to help us now, in exchange for your life?" The man doesn't have to think too long about that one. He agrees to guide David and his army, so they set out again. Soon they come over the brow of a ridge to see the Amalekites below. Listen to how the Bible describes the scene. The Egyptian led David to them. They were scattered all over the place, eating and drinking, gorging themselves on all the loot they had plundered from Philistia and Judah. David pounced. He fought them from before sunrise until evening of the next day. None got away except for four hundred of the younger men who escaped by riding off on camels. David rescued everything the Amalekites had taken. And he rescued his two wives! Nothing and no one was missing—young or old, son or daughter, plunder or whatever. David recovered the whole lot. He herded the sheep and cattle before them, and they all shouted, "David's plunder!" 1 Samuel 30:16-20.

Did you read that? David discovered that every wife, every son, every daughter was still alive! Amazing!

Not even one lamb was gone.

What a victory! In addition to all the recovered goods, David and his army captured an impressive amount of Amalekite goods, so that when they marched back home, there was a surplus. Everyone was praising God. They were shouting, "Look what God gave us!" They came back with more than they had lost. This was the day that David found out that God recovers stolen property. He has a way of getting back what's been ripped off. What the enemy steals, God alone is able to recover.

Why am I telling you this obscure Old Testament story? Because we need to understand that David and his men came to a moment when they chose to get up and go after stolen property. The moment must come for you and me when we say, "Wait a minute—am I just going to keep sitting here feeling bad for myself? In the name of the Lord, my daughter, my son, my grandchild is going to be reclaimed. In the name of the Lord, I am not going to give up on my calling, my potential in life. Satan, you're going to give back that property!"

Remember, we are not wrestling against flesh and blood. We are engaged in spiritual warfare. In your life and mine somebody has to step up and fight for stolen property with the weapons of faith and prayer. You have to say to the devil, "Enough! I'm going to be like David and go after the stolen goods."

Our enemy Satan has no feelings of sympathy. If you don't resist, he'll rip you off every week, all year long. That's his job. But Jesus came that we might have life; *abundant* life.

He can revive your marriage.

He can bring fire back into your soul.

Your spiritual calling can bloom once again.

You can recover the faith that the devil stole. That vibrant heart, faith, and childlike trust in the risen, supernatural Christ; the kind of faith that changes the way you live, talk, and feel.

Satan wants to snatch this more than anything else, for he knows "the righteous will live by faith" (Romans 1:17) and that "without faith it is impossible to please God." (Hebrews 11: 6)

He knows that real faith is our lifeline to God's grace and power. If he can sever the faith connection, he has gained a tremendous victory. He knows that without a living faith, prayer as a force in our lives will be extinguished. We will soon be just mechanically going through the outward forms of religion while experiencing nothing of God's power.

But God can revive fresh faith in our souls if we ask him. He will bring faith alive in us through his Word, as Romans 10:17 declares: "Faith comes by hearing, and hearing by the word of God."

Nothing is impossible with God. In fact, you will see God recover more than you lost, just as David did.

The only question is, do you and I really believe that our God will recover our stolen property? Or do we think our situation is too far-gone for him?

ABOUT THE AUTHOR

Hey there!

I mainly write fantasy and space opera, and you can find all my books in many different ebook stores. You can check out my website for more information about my books, my next projects, and events I'll be attending.

If you enjoyed this book, I'd love your feedback in the form of a review on Amazon or Goodreads.

Thanks for reading!

-Richard

Website: www.richardfierce.com

Facebook: www.facebook.com/dragonfirepress

TikTok: www.tiktok.com/TTPdSrPTBx